ORCHIDS

Orchid

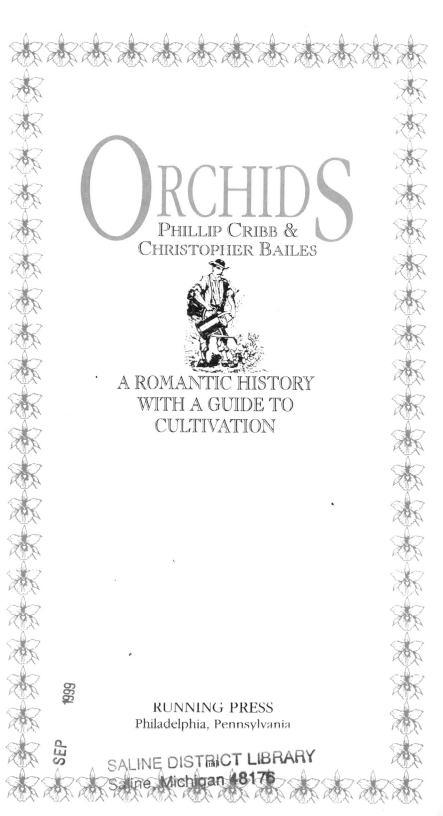

ORCHIDS

PHILLIP CRIBB &
CHRISTOPHER BAILES

A ROMANTIC HISTORY
WITH A GUIDE TO
CULTIVATION

RUNNING PRESS
Philadelphia, Pennsylvania

Copyright © 1992 by Inklink

Concept, design & editorial direction Simon Jennings.
Produced, edited, and designed at Inklink,
Greenwich, London, England.

Text by Phillip Cribb & Christopher Bailes
Designed by Simon Jennings
Botanical illustrations by Julia Cobbold
Archive illustrations enhanced by
Robin Harris & David Day
Edited by Susan Berry

Published in The United States of America
by Running Press, Philadelphia, Pennsylvania

Text setting and computer make-up by Inklink, London.
Image generation by Blackheath Publishing Services, London.
Printed by Southsea International Press, Hong Kong.

Canadian representatives: General Publishing Co., Ltd.,
30 Lesmill Road, Don Mills, Ontario M3B 2T6.
International representatives: Worldwide Media Services, Inc.,
30 Montgomery Street, Jersey City, New Jersey 07302.

9 8 7 6 5 4 3 2 1
Digit on the right indicates the number of this printing.

Library of Congress Catalog Number 92-53692

ISBN 1-56138-142-X

This book may be ordered by mail from the publisher.
Please add $2.50 for postage and handling.
But try your bookstore first!
Running Press Book Publishers
125 South Twenty-Second Street
Philadelphia, Pennsylvania 19103

ORCHIDS
A ROMANTIC HISTORY
WITH A GUIDE TO CULTIVATION
ARRANGED IN THREE CHAPTERS

CONTENTS

THE ORCHID
The aristocrat of the plant world
There are an estimated 25,000 species of orchids which occupy a diversity of habitats from the Arctic tundra to the tropical forests, and from the edges of deserts to the marshes and meadows of Europe and North America.

Introduction

ORCHIDS ARE THE ARISTOCRATS OF THE PLANT WORLD, renowned for the great beauty of their flowers, their exotic origins, and their links with the rich and famous. Yet orchids have never been more accessible to the public than they are today. Orchids can be bought in supermarkets, in corner shops, and on street stalls, as well as in specialist nurseries. Nowadays, orchids are becoming rapidly more popular as house plants, and are no more demanding than the Victorians' aspidistra or Swiss cheese plant (*Monstera*).

The change in the status of orchids during the last century, and particularly over the past 30 years, has largely been the result of improvements in orchid propagation and of a better understanding of cultural requirements. Orchid growing as a hobby is now a truly universal pursuit. It is also an important source of revenue for many countries around the world. In the first section of this book, the rise in popularity of orchids in cultivation is explored, together with a discussion of some of the personalities associated with their introduction, cultivation, and botany.

Undoubtedly a major part of the appeal of orchids lies in their immense diversity of flower form and color. Not only is the orchid family probably the largest in the flowering-plant kingdom, with an estimated 25,000 or more species, but breeders have hybridized orchids extensively over the past 140 years to produce an apparently never-ending supply of novelties. In the second part of this book, readers can gain a foretaste of this diversity and learn something of the background and biology of these strange plants.

The last section introduces the reader to the cultivation of orchids. Advice is given on suitable sources of plants, culture media, pests and diseases, feeding, watering, and propagation to set you on a fascinating and rewarding path as an orchid enthusiast.

DEDICATED TO
OUR ENVIRONMENT
WHICH SUFFERS
IN SILENCE

CHAPTER

I

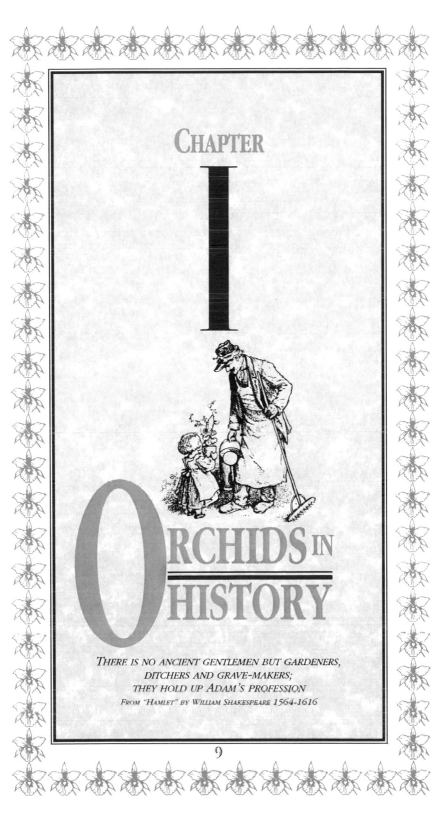

ORCHIDS IN HISTORY

THERE IS NO ANCIENT GENTLEMEN BUT GARDENERS,
DITCHERS AND GRAVE-MAKERS;
THEY HOLD UP ADAM'S PROFESSION
FROM "HAMLET" BY WILLIAM SHAKESPEARE 1564-1616

LIMODORUM GRANDIFLORUM
by Pierre-Joseph Redouté
FROM *LES LILIACÉES* 1816
*This orchid was introduced from China in 1778
and is now known as* PHAIUS TANKERVILLEAE *(see page 37).
Named after Charles Bennet, the fourth Earl of Tankerville
who organized the collection and importation of
orchid species in the 18th century.*

10

ORIGINS OF ORCHID GROWING

ORCHID GROWING IS NOT A MODERN HOBBY. The Chinese were undoubtedly the earliest orchid growers. Orchids have been grown in China for over 2500 years and were mentioned in the *I-Ching*, or Book of Changes, by Confucius (551-479 BC) as being prized for their fragrance and beauty. The species grown then were the small-flowered terrestrial (ground-growing) cymbidiums that remain popular to the present day in China and Japan. The Chinese called these orchids *lan*.

Orchid growing as we know it today is a comparatively recent development. It was stimulated some 200 years ago, firstly by the opening up of the tropical regions of the world by European trade and conquest, and secondly by the evolution of a wealthy class, with time and money to spare for an expensive and esoteric hobby. Empire building was perhaps the stimulus, while the Industrial Revolution provided the wealth. Orchid growing was adopted in England, in particular, by the landed gentry, wealthy industrialists, and royalty.

The earliest records of tropical orchids flowering in cultivation can be traced to the middle of the eighteenth century when a West Indian orchid, *Bletia verecunda*, was sent by Peter Collinson from the Bahamas, and was induced to flower in 1733 by his friend, Mr. Wager. Phillip Miller reported growing *Vanilla planifolia*, the source of commercial vanilla essence, at the Chelsea Physic Garden in London in 1786. By 1794, the Royal Botanic Gardens at Kew could list 15 tropical orchids in cultivation, the first to flower there being the West Indian *Encyclia cochleata* in 1783. From these modest beginnings, the collection at Kew has continued to grow so that, at the present day, some 400 species are cultivated there. It is probably the oldest surviving orchid collection anywhere in the world.

11

ANCIENT & MODERN USES

ORCHIDS HAVE FASCINATED MAN THROUGHOUT HISTORY, but not always for the reasons for which they are grown today. The earliest mention of orchids outside the Orient can be traced to the ancient Greeks, who called them *orchis* and *satyrion*. The latter word has an even more ancient origin in the Near East and is retained to the present day as *Satyrium*, the generic name for a group of Old World terrestrial orchids.

It is, however, the name "orchis" that has been taken up for the family as a whole. Its derivation from the Greek word for a testicle (the shape of the testicular tubers of some orchid species) also demonstrates the use to which the tubers were put by the ancient Greeks. As the early English herbalist William Turner wrote in 1568:

"If the greater roots be eaten of men it maketh men chyldren, and if the roote be eaten of women it maketh women chyldren. And moreove…that women of Thessalia geve it wyth gote's milk to provoke the pleasure of the bodye whylse it is tender, but they geve the dry one to hinder and stop the pleasure of the bodye."

Orchids are still used as aphrodisiacs to the present day in parts of the eastern Mediterranean. In Turkey, orchid tubers are gathered and ground up to form a starchy powder called *salep* – a vital ingredient of "the Aphrodisiac of the Sultans," as sold in the Instanbul spice market. In Southern Africa, the pseudobulbs of the leopard orchid, *Ansellia africana*, are similarly employed as the vital ingredient of an aphrodisiac.

Orchids, by and large, have beautiful flowers and give great pleasure to millions of people, novices, and orchid fanciers alike. The resulting trade in cut flowers and pot plants is worth millions of dollars every year, both in the developed and, increasingly, in the developing world. Already orchids are being grown in some countries as a cash crop to entice farmers away from growing plants for the illegal-drug trade.

Orchids are occasionally used for food and medicines. More than 140 orchid species appear in the Chinese pharmacopoeia, species of genera such as *Gastrodia* and *Dendrobium* being commonly used to treat minor ailments.

12

VANILLA PLANIFOLIA
by Claude Aubriet (1655-1742)
The best-known useful orchid is the Mexican VANILLA PLANIFOLIA, whose seed pods are fermented to produce vanilla essence. It was first used by the Aztecs and other tribes in central America as a flavoring for chocolate drinks for ceremonial occasions. Today, vanilla vines are cultivated in plantations around the world, and are a major foreign-currency earner in Madagascar, Reunion, and Tahiti.

Vanilla flore viridi & albo,
Fructu nigrescente Plum
cum flore

EARLY ORCHID GROWING

DESPITE THEIR EXOTIC FLOWERS and the importation of many thousands of plants from the tropics into Europe in the first half of the nineteenth century, orchids developed a reputation for being hard to grow and difficult to flower. Indeed, England was at that time referred to as the "graveyard of orchids."

The most influential advocates for orchid growing in Victorian England were undoubtedly John Lindley and Joseph Paxton. Lindley, who was Professor of Botany at the University of London and Secretary of the Royal Horticultural Society, wrote extensively on orchids and their cultivation, and is considered the father of orchid taxonomy (classification and nomenclature). However, he was less than successful in the methods he recommended for orchid culture because he mistakenly believed that all orchids grew in the hot and moist tropical lowlands. Paxton, who was the head gardener to the Duke of Devonshire at Chatsworth, adopted a more enlightened view, which Lindley eventually followed. Paxton realized that many orchids grow on trees rather than terrestrially and that many of the more showy species came from the mountain slopes of the tropics and subtropics, preferring cooler, lighter conditions than they had previously received in cultivation. From that point in the middle of the nineteenth century, orchid growing developed from a hobby for the few to a passion for many.

Orchid mania

During the second half of the last century, orchids rapidly gripped the imagination of horticulturists in the British Isles and in Europe, particularly in France, Germany, and Belgium. New orchids fetched high prices, and it became worthwhile for the orchid nurseries to send out their own collectors in search of novelties.

The craze for new orchids made several of the most famous nurseries household names. The earliest in the field were Messrs Loddiges of Hackney, Messrs H. Low of Clapton, and Messrs J. Veitch and Sons of Chelsea and Exeter. Loddiges' nursery supplied John Lindley with many of his new species, but the premature death of George Loddiges led to its sale in the early 1850s. The Low and Veitch establishments flourished until well into the present century as orchid nurseries of excellence. None, however, could match the brilliance of the nursery founded by Frederick Sander in 1876 at St. Albans in Hertfordshire. Sander was a clever grower, an entrepreneur, and a showman. His collectors discovered and sent him some of the finest and most famous of all orchids, including the spectacular *Euanthe* (*Vanda*) *sanderiana* and *Phalaenopsis sanderiana* from the Philippines, *Paphiopedilum sanderianum* from Borneo, and *Odontoglossum sanderianum* from the Andes. Sander's success led to his establishing a second, larger, nursery of 30 acres and 240 glasshouses at Bruges in Belgium, and to his acceptance in the highest circles in Britain and Europe. He gloried in the well-deserved soubriquet of "The Orchid King."

The two world wars also shifted the hub of orchid growing from Europe to the U.S.A. The better climate, particularly in California and Florida, encouraged an impressive orchid industry to develop, with great strides in the breeding of new hybrids. But orchid growing has also become truly internationalized in the past 30 years. In recent years, the rapid growth of tropical-orchid cultivation has been impressive in Japan where there may be as many as 100,000 orchid growers.

Frederick Sander
1847-1920
"The Orchid King"

15

THE ORCHID COLLECTORS

THE SHOWIEST ORCHIDS ARE, BY AND LARGE, TROPICAL and collectors therefore often had to brave long and perilous journeys, dangerous animals, unfriendly locals, debilitating diseases, and the attentions of other collectors. Orchids were dried prior to shipment, and urinating on a rival's cargo was a well-known way of ensuring that the plants would begin to grow during the journey and, consequently, rot before arrival. Despite these problems, some collectors were spectacularly successful.

One of the first of these was the freelance collector Hugh Cuming, who collected in the Philippines in 1835. Among his many discoveries were the moth orchid, *Phalaenopsis aphrodite,* and the sweetly scented *Dendrobium anosmum.*

In 1841, the young Belgian explorer, Jean Linden (1817-98), who had previously traveled widely in the tropical Americas, was hired by a consortium of British orchid growers to collect for them in Venezuela and Colombia. In the Andes, he teamed up with Theodore Hartweg (1812-71), a collector sent out by the Horticultural Society of London. Their prize was the beautiful *Odontoglossum crispum,* which became the most sought-after of all orchids in late Victorian times. Indeed, one plant of the choice clone *O. crispum* 'Fred Sander'

sold for 1500 guineas at a sale in London in the 1890s. This plant had almost been lost in the wild by this time as a result of the stripping of plants and the destruction of the forest by rival collectors. Linden later established his own nursery at Ghent, which rivaled and at times surpassed those of the leading British nurseries of the day. The most famous of all the orchid collectors was probably Joseph von Warscewitz (1812-66), who collected from 1844 onwards in the tropical Americas. His discoveries included some of the most beautiful of all orchids, including the gold-and-purple *Cattleya dowiana* from Costa Rica, the Andean *Cattleya warscewiczii* with its flamboyant pink-and-purple flowers, and the strange slipper orchid *Phragmipedium warscewiczii.*

Whereas most of the nurseries chose to keep their collectors out of the limelight, Frederick Sander (1847-1920) trumpeted the discoveries of his men in the field (although not always very truthfully, as he was as keen as the other nurseries to protect the source of his orchids).

From 1882 onwards, until the start of the First World War in 1914, Sander employed Wilhelm Micholitz as a collector in the Far East. Micholitz kept Sander supplied with a steady stream of choice novelties, but Sander never seemed satisfied, and Micholitz was hounded to discover more. On a famous expedition to New Guinea to find a new white-flowered dendrobium, Micholitz had little success until almost the last day, when he found his quarry growing on a pile of ancestral skulls behind a village. One of those plants of *Dendrobium phalaenopsis* VAR. *schroederianum* was later sold at a London sale room, complete with a skull.

The supply of new and exotic wild orchids began to dry up as the nineteenth century drew to a close, but the nurseries were already enticing their clients with exciting hybrids in colors and shapes undreamed of by mother nature.

Surprise discovery
A white-flowered Dendrobium was discovered in New Guinea growing on a pile of ancestral skulls. A specimen was later sold at a London sale room, complete with skull.

17

THE DIVERSITY OF ORCHIDS

ORCHIDS OCCUPY A GREAT DIVERSITY OF HABITATS from the Arctic Circle to the equator – and as far south as the islands between Australia and New Zealand and the Antarctic. In temperate regions most of the orchids are terrestrial, growing with their roots in the ground like most other plants. However, in tropical countries the competition from other plants on the ground is intense, and in forests, where light, nutrients, and space are at a premium, orchids have literally taken to the trees and are known as epiphytes.

Madagascan epiphyte
An engraving from the turn of the century shows the species ANGRAECUM EBURNEUM *growing on a tree trunk.*

THE ORCHID FAMILY

ORCHIDS ARE ONE OF THE TWO LARGEST FAMILIES of flowering plants, with an estimated 25,000 species. The vast majority of species is found in the tropical regions of the world. The Andes is probably the richest region in the New World. More than 3000 species have so far been recorded in Colombia, and the number increases by dozens every year. In the Old World, the richest regions are probably Borneo (with more than 2000 species) and New Guinea (with probably more than 2500). On one mountain alone, Mount Kinabalu in Sabah, Borneo, a recent survey found more than 700 orchid species.

In contrast, temperate regions are less richly endowed. There are between 150 and 200 species in temperate North America and probably a similar number in Europe, while the British Isles has only 50 native species.

Orchids are an amazingly diverse group of plants. It is difficult to believe that the tiny Australian orchid *Bulbophyllum minutissimum* belongs to the same family as the impressive Indonesian leopard orchid, *Grammatophyllum speciosum*, a large specimen of which can weigh a ton or more.

Not all orchids have large attractive flowers. Indeed, most orchids have rather small flowers, and grotesque blooms are as common as attractive ones. Some orchid flowers, such as those of *Oberonia* or *Phreatia*, are miniscule while the largest, such as those of *Paphiopedilum rothschildianum*, can be 12in (30cm) across.

With some orchids, notably in genera such as *Catasetum* and *Cycnoches* (swan orchids), two or even three types of flowers can be found in the same species. When this occurs, the different flowers are male, female or hermaphrodite.

Many orchids are primary colonizers of disturbed habitats. In such places, the competition from other plants is low and the orchid's unique relationship with its own fungus gives it a distinct advantage in its growth rate. The orchid-fungus link is called a "mycorrhizal relationship" (see page 24).

HYBRID ORCHIDS

IN 1854, THE ENTERPRISING ORCHID GROWER, John Dominy, of Messrs Veitch and Sons of Chelsea, flowered *Calanthe dominyi*, the first artificially raised hybrid orchid. This proved to be a milestone in orchid development, because orchids were quickly found to be fairly promiscuous and within limits species could be hybridized readily to produce novel forms. The nurseries realized that improvements in vigor, flower shape, flower texture, and longevity could result from these crossings. Furthermore, the orchid-growing public's desire for novelty was seemingly never-ending.

There are about 20 major breeding groups of orchid that go to make up the bulk of all orchid hybrids available today. The most important of these are based around the following genera and their close relatives: *Paphiopedilum, Cymbidium, Cattleya, Odontoglossum, Vanda,* and *Phalaenopsis.*

A second development, however, ensured the future of the orchid industry and brought orchids to a far wider audience – the development of laboratory methods for propagating orchids. The discoveries of the French botanist Noel Bernard at the beginning of this century, and subsequent developments by the German Hans Burgeff, the American Lewis Knudsen, and the Frenchman Georges Morel, were critical to the evolution of the mass production of orchids. Bernard discovered the mycorrhizal association of orchids and demonstrated that orchids could grow from seed only if the seeds were penetrated by a fungal hypha. Burgeff showed that the seed of orchids could be germinated in test tubes, provided the correct fungus was also present. In the late 1930s, Knudsen identified the nutrients that the orchid derived from the fungus and, by providing these in a nutrient medium, enabled growers to germinate orchid seed in test tubes without a fungus present. Because each seed pod can produce thousands of seeds, this discovery opened the way to less expensive orchids.

ORCHID NAMES

BECAUSE MOST ORCHIDS ORIGINATE in tropical countries, few have been given vernacular English names. Most names used for orchids are bipartite and latinized.

The first term is a genus name, such as *Cattleya*, *Dendrobium* or *Odontoglossum,* of which the first letter is capitalized. The second term is usually an adjective, such as *sylvestris, violacea* or *sanderianum,* which agrees in gender with the generic name that precedes it. The initial letter of the second term is usually lower case. Thus in the genus *Odontoglossum* you may find several species such as *Odontoglossum crispum, Odontoglossum nobile* and *Odontoglossum hallii*. Species in the same genus are considered to be related more closely to each other than to species in other genera. Species names are usually printed in italics.

Hybrid names are usually tripartite. As with species, the first term is a generic name. However, because some hybrids have more than one genus in their parentage the first term may be the name of a hybrid genus such as *Laeliocattleya* (a hybrid of *Laelia* and *Cattleya*). The second term is the grex name, the name of the group of hybrids all having the same parentage. Grex adjectives can be one to three words long and are vernacular names, as opposed to Latin ones. *Cymbidium* Mavourneen Jester and *Odontoglossum* Eric Young are both names of grexes. A listing of all registered grexes is kept by the Orchid Registrar of the Royal Horticultural Society, which is the recognized registration authority for hybrid orchids. The third term is the cultivar name which, like the grex name, is a vernacular word or short phrase. To distinguish it from the grex name, it is placed in single inverted commas, for example 'St. Helier', 'Jester', and 'Showgirl' are all cultivar names used in *Cymbidium*. Hybrid names can, therefore, be rather lengthy.

CONSERVATION AND THE LAW

MANY ORCHIDS ARE NOW RARE IN THEIR NATIVE HABITATS or even threatened with extinction. A few, indeed, may even be extinct already. The southern Indian *Paphiopedilum druryi*, for example, was collected to extinction in the late 1970s.

National and state governments in many countries have sought to protect their rare plants, and numerous species are protected by legislation from being dug up or picked in the wild. Nature reserves and protected areas also give considerable protection to the plants that grow within their boundaries. Orchid growers should, by and large, avoid buying plants collected in the wild. Not only are these often difficult to establish, but buying them encourages further depredations on wild populations. Nursery-raised plants are usually easier to establish and often have better flowers, as they are frequently grown from selected parent clones.

The Convention of International Trade in Endangered Species of Wild Fauna and Flora legislation (CITES) has been adopted by more than 100 countries. This controls the export and import of orchids in those countries that are signatories. All orchids are covered by the legislation and orchid plants that are traded internationally must be accompanied by the appropriate CITES documents. However, from 1992, all orchid seedlings in flasks are exempt and do not need CITES documents.

CHAPTER

II

ORCHIDS FOR YOUR HOUSE & GARDEN

WHERE THERE ARE FLOWERS ABOUT,
THE HOSTESS APPEARS GLAD,
THE CHILDREN PLEASED,
THE VERY DOG AND CAT GRATEFUL
FOR OUR ARRIVAL

FROM "RUSTIC ADORNMENTS FOR HOMES OF TASTE"
SHIRLEY HIBBERD 1856

THE LIFE CYCLE OF AN ORCHID

THE LIFE CYCLE OF THE ORCHID illustrates how complex relationships between organisms can be. Orchids have dustlike seeds containing an embryo of a hundred or so cells, enclosed in a covering called a testa. Orchid seeds have no built-in food store and have, therefore, developed a different strategy for survival. To germinate, an orchid seed needs to be penetrated by the threads of a particular fungus, termed a mycorrhiza. The orchid embryo reacts to the fungal penetration by dissolving the fungus with enzymes and utilizing the released nutrients. This method of obtaining food often appears to be very efficient and some orchids have been known to flower from seed in a matter of 18 months by this means.

Most orchids' dependence upon the fungal partner is limited to the few weeks that it takes for the developing orchid to produce its first green leaves. The leaves then take over production of essential food for the growing seedling. In some orchids, however, green leaves are never produced, and all of the plant's food comes from the associated fungus. These orchids are usually referred to as saprophytes. One of these is the bird's-nest orchid, *Neottia nidus-avis*, a common European orchid of beech woods, which only appears above ground at flowering time. The whole process of development of the flowering shoot, flowering, pollination, and fruiting takes place in a matter of weeks in the spring.

The most extraordinary saprophytic orchids are the two Australian underground orchids, *Rhizanthella gardneri* from Western Australia and *R. slateri* from Eastern Australia. These complete their life cycle below the ground, edging to the surface only to flower. The inflorescences grow from an undergrown tuberlike organ and push the surface leaf litter aside with their bracts to allow small flies to enter to pollinate the flowers. Both species are very rare and have seldom been seen. Indeed, the first discoveries of both were entirely accidental.

Orchid pollination can be just as strange and specific as the germination of the seeds. Most orchids are cross-pollinated by insects that are attracted to their flowers. The relationship between orchid and pollinator is thought to be rather specific. Insects are the most prolific organisms on earth and, consequently, orchids have a wonderfully diverse choice of pollinators. The rapid evolution of orchids into so many species is thought to be a result of pollinator specificity.

Pollination in orchids can be quite bizarre. Charles Darwin was one of the first biologists to be attracted to study the strange pollination biology of the orchids. Take the bucket orchid, *Coryanthes macrantha*, which has a remarkable large flower, with the lip divided into three parts. The basal part possesses two glands that secrete a syrupy liquid. The central part separates the base from the bucket-shaped part, which acts as a receptacle. Potential pollinating bees are attracted to the secretion on the glands, become drunk on the rich liquid, and fall into the bucket, thereby wetting their wings. Unable to fly out of the bucket, they swim to the only exit beneath the column apex bearing the pollen masses. These are removed as the bee squeezes beneath them. Pollination is effected when the bee repeats the procedure at another flower.

The pollination of some European bee orchids of the genus *Ophrys* is even more remarkable. These have flowers that mimic bees and wasps, hence their common name. Not only do humans think they look like bees, but so do male bees of particular species. The flowers emit a scent similar to that of the female bees and this entices the males to visit the flowers. When a male lands, the flower feels like a female bee, and excites copulatory movements from the male visitor. In the course of this behavior, the pollen masses are picked up by the bee and transferred to another flower, where the male bee repeats his foolhardy and futile copulation.

WHAT IS AN ORCHID?

ORCHIDS ARE FLOWERING PLANTS that are characterized by simple but highly evolved flowers, their modifications being linked to highly specialized modes of cross-pollination. All orchids have their flower parts in threes, much like those of lilies, tulips, and other related plants. The outer, showier parts of the flower are called the sepals and petals, and orchid flowers have three of each. In its outer segments, the orchid flower is not very different from other flowers, but the sepals and petals enclose the sexual parts of the flowers and, in orchids, these are quite distinctive.

The orchid plant

Orchids can be broadly divided into those that grow on the ground (terrestrials) and those that grow on trees or rocks (epiphytes). The former predominate in temperate regions and in the tropical grasslands and marshes. However, in the forests of the tropics and subtropics, epiphytes outnumber terrestrial orchids.

Epiphytic orchids have several characteristic features associated with their habitat. Epiphytes in the tropical forest may well receive quantities of water every day but the hot sun soon dries them out. As a result, they need to protect their water supplies to survive. Consequently, many species have swollen stems called pseudobulbs, and fleshy or leathery leaves; both features are associated with water conservation. Epiphytic orchids also have stout roots that assume a silvery appearance because the outer layers, termed the velamen, consist of dead cells which protect the sensitive inner tissue. Many tropical epiphytes, especially those of seasonal forests and woodlands, have to survive periods of drought and may lose their leaves at this time, producing new ones during the next wet season.

Terrestrial orchids also have to survive periods of adverse weather, such as drought or freezing conditions. They often do so by producing underground storage organs, such as tubers or rhizomes, which sprout anew as the weather improves.

THE SEPALS

These are the outermost organs and can be attractively colored like petals, but are more usually less brightly colored. Their function is to protect the sexual parts of the flower as the bud develops.

THE PETALS

Orchid petals are usually the most attractively colored floral segments, the upper two being similar, but the lower one often quite different in shape, ornamentation and patterning.

DORSAL SEPAL

COLUMN

PETAL

PETAL

LATERAL SEPAL

SEXUAL ORGANS

Most flowers have three or more ANTHERS shedding the POLLEN (male sex cells) and surrounding the separate ovary, which comprises one to several CARPELS surmounted by a STYLE with a STIGMA at the apex. Pollen falling on the stigma germinates and the male sex cells eventually fertilize the OVULES (female sex cells). In orchids, the sexual organs are highly modified, the male and female organs being fused into a stalklike column, and much reduced in number. Most orchids have a single anther, and the stigma resides on the under surface of the column beneath the anther. The pollen is not dustlike but is united into a discrete number of masses called POLLINIA. Most orchids have two, four, six or eight pollinia.

THE LIP OR LABELLUM

This segment acts as a landing platform for pollinators. The lip often has more or less complex projections on its surface that function as "landing lights" for pollinators and has a spur at the base to attract nectar-seeking insects.

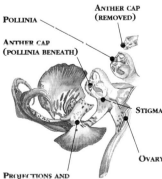

POLLINIA

ANTHER CAP (REMOVED)

ANTHER CAP (POLLINIA BENEATH)

STIGMA

OVARY

PROJECTIONS AND MARKINGS TO GUIDE POLLINATING INSECTS TO COLUMN

27

TROPICAL AMERICAN ORCHIDS

THE TROPICAL AMERICAS CAN BOAST THE RICHEST diversity of wild orchids, including many of the most spectacular species in genera such as *Cattleya, Laelia, Odontoglossum, Oncidium,* and *Sophronitis*. The three richest areas are Central America from Mexico to Panama, the Andean chain from Venezuela and Colombia south to Bolivia, and the mountains of eastern Brazil. Many of the showiest hybrids derive from species found in these areas. Such has been the overcollection and forest destruction that many species are now threatened with extinction in their native habitats.

PHRAGMIPEDIUM CAUDATUM

Slipper orchids

Slipper orchids are among the most popular of all orchids in cultivation. The largest genus in the tropical Americas is *Phragmipedium,* with about 15 species. *Phragmipedium caudatum*, one of the best-known species and one of the most widespread, is found in the mountains from Mexico south to Peru. A strange, close relative, *Phragmipedium lindenii*, lacks the slipper-shaped lip that is characteristic of all other slipper ochids.

Phragmipedium besseae
One of the most extraordinary discoveries of recent years was that in 1979 of P. BESSEAE, the only slipper orchid that has scarlet flowers. It grows at 4000-5000ft (1300-1500m) on the almost vertical cliffs of rivers that flow off the eastern slopes of the Andes in Peru and Ecuador. The first hybrids of P. BESSEAE are just beginning to appear and presage fresh interest in this remarkable genus.

PHRAGMIPEDIUM BESSEAE

Masdevallia & its allies

Masdevallias are small to medium-sized orchids abundant in the Andes from Bolivia to Venezuela. Popular in late Victorian times, they have undergone a resurgence of interest in recent years. Species such as the Peruvian *Masdevallia veitchiana*, with scarlet flowers suffused with purple papillae, and *M. coccinea*, which can have purple, yellow or white flowers, have always been coveted by orchid collectors. The more delicately colored species, such as *M. caudata* from Colombia and Venezuela, also deserve a place in any collection as they produce large flowers in abundance on small plants.

The allied Andean genus *Dracula*, including the alarmingly named *D. vampira*, is also popular in cultivation and is generally grown in hanging baskets so that the pendent flowers can develop. The triangular flowers are usually somberly colored deep purple to black on a yellow background; each segment has a long tail.

Terrestrial orchids

Tropical American terrestrial orchids are not often seen in cultivation, although many deserve more attention. Ground orchids, such as the red-flowered *Stenorrhynchus speciosus* and the purple-flowered bletias, are easy to grow and flower. However, more frequently seen is the clump-forming *Sobralia macrantha*, which develops 3–4in (9–11cm) cattleya-like purple flowers, with yellow throats, at the end of bamboo-like leafy canes that reach 3ft (1m) or more long. It is a common orchid on river banks, low down on forest trees, and on roadsides in the mountains of Mexico and Central America.

MASDEVALLIA VEITCHIANA

MASDEVALLIA CAUDATA

SOBRALIA MACRANTHA

29

Odontoglossum crispum
This orchid from the Andes of southern and central Colombia is now rare in the wild. It grows at the edges of mist-forest patches at between 8000 and 9000ft (2300 and 2800m). It is a variable species with sprays of large, flat white flowers, variously spotted with purple on the segments and yellow on the lip. Selected clones collected towards the end of the last century fetched high prices in the London sales rooms.

30

Odontoglossum alliance

Odontoglossums and their allies are among the most charming of orchids, with large but delicate flowers, often borne in long sprays. *Odontoglossum* itself is a genus of about 60 species, mainly concentrated in the Andes from Venezuela and Colombia to Peru. Another prized species is the closely allied *O. nobile* (also called *O. pescatorei*) with slightly smaller, scented flowers, distinguished by their broader lip.

LEMBOGLOSSUM ROSSII

Several genera, notably *Lemboglossum, Rossioglossum,* and *Odontoglossum,* now considered distinct, were formerly included in *Odontoglossum. Lemboglossum* is a genus of some 15 species from the mountain forests of Mexico and Central America. *Lemboglossum rossii* from Mexico, Guatemala, Honduras, and Nicaragua is a pretty dwarf species with spikes of two to four white to rose-pink flowers, blotched with brown on the bases of the sepals and petals. It is found growing as an epiphyte in the mist forests at 6500-8000ft (2000-2400m). Another Mexican species is the spectacular *Rossioglossum grande* with several large yellow-and-chestnut flowers. Slightly smaller is *R. insleayi,* also from Mexico, which has larger flowers. It was discovered in Mexico by John Ross in 1838.

ROSSIOGLOSSUM INSLEAYI

The dividing line between *Odontoglossum* and the far larger genus *Oncidium* has been the cause of much debate. *Oncidium* is widespread in the tropical Americas. *Oncidium luridum* is found almost throughout the genus. Its large leathery leaves are characteristic of a group called the "mule-eared oncidiums." Its 1-1$\frac{1}{2}$in (3-4cm) flowers are not showy, but are borne in sprays that can reach 6ft (2m) long.

ONCIDIUM LURIDUM

31

CATTLEYA AMETHYSTOGLOSSA

LAELIA SPECIOSA

RHYNCHOLAELIA DIBYANA

The Cattleya alliance

Cattleya is the showiest of a group of related orchid genera from tropical America that hybridize fairly easily in cultivation. For many people, cattleyas are the archetypal orchid, with large showy purple, pink or white flowers that verge on the vulgar. The species are, however, usually less blowsy than the hybrids and are rewarding subjects. *Cattleya amethystoglossa,* from the eastern Brazilian states of Espiritu Santo and Bahia, where it grows on rocks and on palm trees in sunny positions, was introduced into cultivation in 1860. It can grow to 3ft (1m) tall, but is usually shorter. A well-grown specimen can have trusses of 30 attractive 4in (10cm) wide flowers.

Laelia speciosa is a Mexican species that is found as an epiphyte in the oak forests of the central mountains at altitudes up to 8000ft (2400m). Its smallish plant bears one or two large rose-pink flowers. In Mexico, it is gathered for religious festivals.

Rhyncholaelia dibyana has large greenish-cream flowers with a characteristic fringed lip; these features have led to it being used to produce some attractive hybrids. It is found in Mexico, Belize, and Honduras and was one of the earliest orchids introduced from that area into Britain, flowering for Edward St.Vincent Digby of Dorset in 1845.

Epidendrum is the largest genus in this alliance, with several hundred species, many of which are to be found in cultivation. Few, however, can match the splendor of cattleyas and laelias. The Central American *E. pseudepidendrum* is an exception because of its unusually colored, long-lasting flowers, with green sepals and petals, a purple apex to the column, and a bright tangerine lip.

Bucket orchids & their allies

Some of the strangest of all orchids are those in the genera *Coryanthes, Catasetum, Mormodes,* and their allies. Many of these have strangely shaped flowers, and some have flowers of two or occasionally even three sorts in the same species. *Catasetum pileatum,* found in the forests of the basins of the Upper Amazon and Orinoco, is a beautiful orchid with male flowers that have a relatively flat cream-colored lip up to 4in (10cm) across. The female flowers are smaller, with the lip uppermost in the flower. The male flowers have two long antennae at the base of the column. A pollinating bee touching these antennae triggers an explosive release of the pollen masses onto its back.

Bucket orchids belong to the genus *Coryanthes. Coryanthes speciosa* is one of the commoner species, widespread in the tropical Americas in dense forests, up to 3000ft (1000m).

Less elaborate but well-worth cultivating are the various species of *Stanhopea,* which have pendent inflorescences of two or more fleshy, strongly scented flowers that will perfume an entire glasshouse. *Stanhopea saccata,* from Mexico, Guatemala, and El Salvador, has flowers up to 4in (10cm) long. It is one of the rarer wild species of epiphyte, in forests up to 4500ft (1400m).

CATASETUM PILEATUM

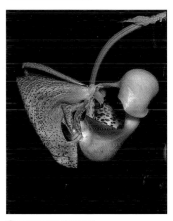

CORYANTHES SPECIOSA

STANHOPEA SACCATA

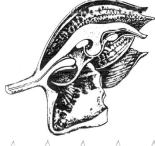

33

LYCASTE SKINNERI (L. VIRGINALIS)

MAXILLARIA PUMILA

PESCATOREA LEHMANNII

Lycaste & its allies

Another large group of tropical American orchids centers on the genera *Maxillaria* and *Lycaste*. Many maxillarias have relatively small and not very brightly colored flowers. *Maxillaria pumila* from the West Indies has small purple flowers, whereas *M. Sanderiana* has far larger white flowers with purple markings.

Few orchids have excited the orchid world as much as *Lycaste skinneri,* also known as *L. virginalis*, nowadays a great rarity from the rain forests of southern Mexico, Guatemala, El Salvador, and Honduras. In most places it has been collected to extinction. It was discovered in Guatemala by George Ure Skinner, who sent living plants to James Bateman. Bateman first flowered it in 1840. It has large white or pale-rose flowers, with a deeper rose-pink lip. The rare albino variety is particularly sought after. The golden-flowered lycastes, such as *L. aromatica* and *L. cruenta*, are common in cultivation and produce spicily scented flowers every year.

Neomoorea wallisii has up to 12 cupped orange-brown flowers, up to 2in (6cm) across and with a white-and-yellow lip marked with dark-maroon veins, in an erect spike. Its leaves can reach more than 3ft (1m) long. It is found growing at low altitudes as an epiphyte or as a semi-terrestrial in forests in Colombia and Panama.

Another attractive ally is *Pescatorea lehmannii*, with flowers 3in (8cm) broad , whose name also commemorates two orchidologists, the wealthy French orchid grower Jean-Paul Pescatore and the German collector and diplomat Frederick Lehmann. Lehmann discovered it in Colombia growing as an epiphyte.

TROPICAL ASIATIC ORCHIDS

THE TROPICAL FORESTS OF ASIA are home to a rich array of orchids, including some of the most popular groups such as moth orchids (*Phalaenopsis*), buttonhole orchids (*Cymbidium*), and slipper orchids (*Paphiopedilum*). Many of the earliest introductions of tropical species to Europe came from India, particularly from the foothills of the massive Himalayan chain, and from the East Indies islands of Java, Sumatra, and Borneo.

Slipper orchids

The tropical Asiatic slipper orchids belonging to the genus *Paphiopedilum* are among the most popular of all orchids. The 70 or so species are distributed from India to the Philippines, New Guinea, and the Solomon Islands. Many species have been cultivated for more than 150 years, yet some of the most attractive examples, such as the golden-flowered *Paphiopedilum armeniacum* from southern China, are comparatively recent discoveries. Closely allied to it is the bubble-gum orchid, *Paphiopedilum micranthum*, also from China. This grows on limestone outcrops and cliffs in the wild. Both have tessellated dark-and-light-green leaves, heavily purple-spotted on the underside, and are unusual in having runners from which new growths develop.

One of the most famous of all orchids is *Paphiopedilum rothschildianum*, named after Baron Ferdinand Rothschild, the eminent Victorian orchid grower. It is a rarity in the wild, being confined to one or two localities in northern Borneo, where it grows on steep cliffs in the shade. It carries three to six large cream-and-purple flowers on each spike.

PAPHIOPEDILUM MICRANTHUM

PAPHIOPEDILUM ROTHSCHILDIANUM

Paphiopedilum hirsutissimum
This well-known species of slipper orchid from northeast India, Burma, Thailand, and southwest China that has been in cultivation since the middle of the last century. It has solitary but large flowers, the purple spatula-shaped petals standing out horizontally.

36

Terrestrial species

Some of the first Asiatic orchids to arrive in Europe were the Chinese terrestrial species, such as *Phaius tankervilleae*. This is a large plant that can grow to over 3ft (1m) tall and has erect spikes of showy brown flowers with a purple trumpet-shaped lip.

Spathoglottis plicata is one of the commonest Asiatic orchids and a colonizer of disturbed areas. It is found throughout southeast Asia and the islands across to the southwest Pacific; and where it does not occur naturally, it has often been introduced. It usually has several bright-purple or pink flowers at the top of a tall spike that can reach 3ft (1m) in height. Part of its success is that it is often self-pollinating. Several allied species are also cultivated, although less frequently, including the yellow-flowered *S. aurea* from Malaya and the permanganate-flowered *S. petri* from Vanuatu.

Necklace orchids

Many species of the genus *Coelogyne*, and its allies such as *Pholidota, Chelonistele,* and *Dendrochilum,* are well worth growing for their delicate flowers, which are often borne in profusion in arching or hanging chains. The best known of these necklace orchids are species such as the southeast Asian *C. massangeana* and *C. dayana* which have pendent spikes of dozens of cream flowers marked with chocolate brown on the lip.

The green-and-black flowered *C. pandurata*, from the swamp forests of Borneo, Sumatra, and Malaya, has long been a favorite in collections. In an arching inflorescence, it has several large bright-green flowers with jet-black markings on the fiddle-shaped lip.

PHAIUS TANKERVILLEAE

SPATHOGLOTTIS PLICATA

COELOGYNE PANDURATA

37

DENDROBIUM NOBILE

DENDROBIUM PENDULUM (D. CRASSINODE)

DENDROBIUM BRYMERIANUM

Dendrobiums

Dendrobiums were grown by the Chinese some 2500 years ago. *Dendrobium* is a large Old World genus of perhaps 900 species distributed throughout tropical and subtropical Asia, the Malay Archipelago, the south Pacific islands, and Australasia. Today, there are two main types of *Dendrobium* in cultivation: soft-cane species and hybrids which derive from mainland Asiatic species, and hard-cane species that derive from brilliant purple-flowered *Dendrobium biggibbum*, from New Guinea and northeastern Australia, and the species allied to *Dendrobium antennatum* from the same regions.

The best-known mainland Asiatic species is *Dendrobium nobile,* found from northeastern India across to southern China and Indo-China. In some areas it is used medicinally; and in Arunchal Pradesh, in India, it is revered as sacred. It has large, wide, flat flowers of purple and white with a trumpet-shaped lip and a dark-purple mark in the throat. It was hybridized with allied species, and these form the basis of the popular modern Yamamoto hybrids.

Dendrobium pendulum (also known as *D. crassinode*) is not unlike *D. nobile* in its flower shape, but has characteristic stems with swollen nodes. Its fragrant 2in (5cm) flowers have white sepals and petals with pink to magenta tips and a similarly marked velvety lip, with a large orange-yellow mark in the throat. It is widespread in southeast Asia.

Dendrobium brymerianum from India, Burma, and Thailand is one of the many golden-flowered species and is characterized by its long-fringed petals and lip. Its perfumed flowers are held flat and can be 3in (8cm) across.

38

Bulbophyllums

The only genus larger than *Dendrobium* in the Old World tropics is *Bulbophyllum,* with an estimated 1500 species. One of the best large-flowered species is *B. lobbii.* In the wild it grows in a variety of habitats, but usually as an epiphyte on the trunks and larger branches of rain-forest trees. It is easy to grow and flowers prolifically

BULBOPHYLLUM LOBBII

Buttonhole orchids

The most widely grown of all orchids are the cymbidiums, which are grown for buttonholes and sprays and as pot plants. The genus comprises about 50 species distributed from the Himalayas eastwards to China and Japan, and south through the Malay Archipelago to New Guinea and Australia. The 10 or so species that produce large flowers are predominantly Himalayan, and these have been used to produce some spectacular hybrids. The main species involved in breeding programs have been *Cymbidium lowianum, C. hookerianum* and *C. iridioides,* all in shades of green, yellow, and brown, and the white-flowered *C. insigne* and *C. eburneum.*

Cymbidium eburneum, from the eastern Himalayas, southern China, and Thailand has one to three inflorescences of white flowers, 3-5in (8-12cm) across. The lip is prettily marked with distictive pink or pale purple spotting.

Crossing large-flowered hybrids with some of the small-flowered species has produced the miniature hybrids used as pot plants nowadays. A reliable one is the well-known *Cymbidium* 'Showgirl.'

CYMBIDIUM INSIGNE

CYMBIDIUM EBURNEUM

39

VANDA TRICOLOR

EUANTHE SANDERIANA

PHALAENOPSIS VIOLACEA

Vandas, moth orchids, & their allies

The genus *Vanda*, comprising about 40 species, is distributed from the Himalayas and India through tropical Asia to the Philippines, New Guinea, the Solomon Islands, and Australia. Perhaps its most celebrated member is the blue vanda, *Vanda coerulea,* discovered by William Griffith in 1837. It is an epiphyte that grows in open forest at between 2500 and 5500ft (800 and 1700m). Wild plants have pale-blue tessellated flowers 3-4in (7-10cm) across.

Another common species is *Vanda tricolor,* from Java and Bali, and its variety *suavis.* The typical variety was introduced to Europe by Thomas Lobb in 1846. Each inflorescence bears 6 to 10 fragrant flowers, 2-3in (5-7cm) across. Vandas need to be grown in light conditions to flower well.

The Philippine species *Euanthe sanderiana,* often considered a vanda, has flatter, more substantial flowers, than *V. coerulea,* reaching 5in (12cm) across. It has pink flowers with golden lower segments veined with red and a red-brown lip.

The most popular of the vanda allies are the moth orchids of the genus *Phalaenopsis* of which there are some 45 species. The best known are the closely allied *P. amabilis* from the Malay Archipelago and *P. aphrodite* from the Philippines. Both have sprays of large, flat snow-white flowers with yellow and red markings on a relatively small lip. They grow in the rain forest, often on trees overhanging water. The similar but pink-flowered Philippines species, *P. schilleriana* and *P. sanderiana,* have been important parents in hybridizing programs with the white-flowered species.

Both have silvery mottled leaves. Another group of *Phalaenopsis* have fleshier stellate flowers. These include the rare Bornean *P. gigantea,* whose leaves can reach 3ft (1m) long. Its pendent spikes contain as many as 30 flowers, each 2in (5cm) across. It is nearing extinction because its habitat is being destroyed by logging. *P. violacea* is also in this group, and has an erect but short inflorescence that stands proud of the leaves and carries purple scented flowers.

Many of the smaller-flowered orchids related to *Vanda* are also eagerly cultivated. The rare southeast Asian orchid *Renanthera imschootiana* has sprays of crimson-red flowers that can reach 18in (45cm) long.

Rhynchostylis is another small genus of a few species, but one that can be found in many collections. *Rhynchostylis gigantea,* is a medium-sized plant that produces bottlebrush-like inflorescences of fragrant white flowers spotted with pink. A well-grown plant can produce up to 20 flower spikes with more than 1000 flowers. Attractive varieties with deep-purple or pure-white flowers are particularly sought after. It is found growing epiphytically in the seasonal woodlands and forests of Thailand, Burma, and Indo-China.

Another small-flowered species that is popular in cultivation is *Gastrochilus calceolaris,* which has short inflorescences of clustered flowers with greenish or yellowish sepals and petals, blotched with brown, and a white lip marked with yellow and red. It is widespread in the Himalayas, from Nepal eastwards to Malaya.

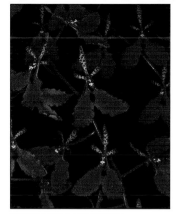

RENANTHERA IMSCHOOTIANA

RHYNCHOSTYLIS GIGANTEA

GASTROCHILUS CALCEOLARIS

41

The leopard orchid
The orchid's long leafy canes produce branched flowering spikes of yellow flowers, variously spotted with deep maroon. Pure-yellow or deep-maroon flowered forms are prized by growers. The leopard orchid was discovered by John Ansell on the island of Fernando Po in 1841 and John Lindley named the genus in his honor.

42

AFRICAN & MADAGASCAN ORCHIDS

A FRICA IS RELATIVELY POOR IN ORCHID SPECIES, in compari-
son with the tropical Americas and Asia. Even so, it
has nearly 2000 species and a far higher proportion of
terrestrials which grow in the seasonally flooded grasslands of tropical Africa and the drier scrub and grasslands
of southern Africa. Most of the epiphtyes are tropical, but
a few extend into South Africa, particularly in the forests
of the Transvaal and Natal. Madagascar is almost as rich
in orchids as Africa. Most of its orchids are endemic, and
some are very popular indeed.

Terrestrial species

The largest and most abundant
terrestrial orchids in Africa and
Madagascar belong to the genera
*Eulophia, Habenaria, Cynorkis,
Satyrium,* and *Disa.* Of these, the
Disa species from the Cape are
particularly popular and grow vig-
orosly in acidic composts ranging
from pure sphagnum to lime-free
sand. The finest species is without
doubt the Pride of Table
Mountain, *Disa uniflora,* which
grows to about 16in (40cm) tall
and can have two to four large,
scarlet flowers. It is a protected
orchid in the wild, growing in
seepages over rocks or along the
sides of mountain streams.

Hybrids of *Disa uniflora* with
D. tripetaloides, D. cardinalis, and
other allied species are widely
grown and flower freely in the
right conditions.

The best known of the epiphytic orchids of Africa is the leopard
orchid, *Ansellia africana* (left). It
is the closest relative to the Asiatic
cymbidiums. Leopard orchids are
frequently found growing on
woodland trees inland and on the
Doum palm near the coast, where
it is a favorite perch for mambas
and other snakes.

DISA UNIFLORA

DISA CARDINALIS

EULOPHIELLA ROEMPLERIANA

GRAPHORKIS SCRIPTA

ANGRAECUM MAGDALENAE

Madagascan epiphytes

Madagascar can boast many spectacular epiphytic species, such as *Eulophiella roempleriana* with large pink flowers, *Cymbidiella pardalina* with green-and-red flowers spotted with black, and *Grammangis ellisii,* which resembles in many ways a large leopard orchid. *Graphorkis scripta* is related to the larger-flowered *Grammangis ellisii* and to the African leopard orchid, *Ansellia africana.* It is an epiphyte found in Madagascar, the Mascarene Islands, and the Seychelles. However, its most famous orchids are the *Aerangis* and *Angraecum* species. The best known of these is *Angraecum sesquipedale,* the comet orchid, which will always be associated with Charles Darwin. It has large star-shaped creamy-white flowers with a spur 12in (30cm) long at the base of the lip. Darwin predicted that the flowers would be pollinated by a hawk moth with a tongue 12in (30cm) long. Forty years later, the moth was discovered, confirming Darwin's prediction.

Closely related to the comet orchid is another Madagascan orchid, *Angraecum magdalenae.* This also has large, white flowers, with a slender spur 4in (10cm) long, and is almost certainly also moth-pollinated. In the wild, it grows in large colonies on rocks in the mountains. Its most characteristic feature is its swordlike bilaterally flattened leaves that are borne in a fan on a short stem. Madagascar has many other angraecums, and there are another 30 or so in tropical Africa, which are mostly less showy.

AUSTRALIAN ORCHIDS

A USTRALIA HAS A PECULIAR AND RICH ORCHID FLORA of more than 1000 species, which is particularly rich in terrestrial forms. Australia's isolation has led to the evolution of many strange orchids, particularly in the eastern, southeastern, and southwestern margins of the country. The strangest of all Australian orchids are the underground orchids, *Rhizanthella gardneri* and *R. slateri,* whose entire life is spent beneath the ground's surface.

Australian epiphytes

Epiphytic and lithophytic orchids are mainly confined to the wetter, eastern margins of the continent, with a few species such as the tough *Cymbidium canaliculatum* also found in the north. The largest genus is *Dendrobium,* with perhaps 40 species in Australia, many being endemic. One of these, and arguably the finest, is the rock lily, *D. speciosum,* which can form a massive plant with thick pseudobulbs, bearing a few leathery leaves at the top and arching sprays of 30 to 50 fragrant cream or white flowers, 2-3in (5 7cm) long. Like many of the Australian species, it likes to grow in rather exposed situations, on sandstone rocks in the wild, and will not flower well in cultivation if grown in shaded conditions. *Dendrobium kingianum* is closely related to *D. speciosum* but is altogether more slender, with rose-pink flowers.

Australia also has some vanda relatives in its flora, although most have far smaller flowers than their showy Asiatic relatives. The genus *Sarcochilus,* with some 15 endemic species, has some very attractive members, and some of these have been hybridized. One of the easiest species in cultivation is *S. hartmannii* (see page 46) from southeast Queensland and northern New South Wales.

CYMBIDIUM CANALICULATUM

DENDROBIUM KINGIANUM

Sarcochilus hartmannii
This orchid grows on escarpments, cliffs, and boulders up to 3000ft (1000m). Its attractive flat white flowers, about 1in (3cm) across, are prettily speckled with red at the base of the sepals and petals.

Ground orchids

The main terrestrial genera in Australia are the greenhoods (*Pterostylis*), sun orchids (*Thelymitra*), and spider orchids (*Caladenia*). They all grow in nutrient poor, acidic conditions in the forests, woods, and marshes of the country. Some of the green-hoods are among the easiest species to grow in cultivation, especially those that naturally form colonies. In pots, they will often proliferate rapidly and need regular repotting.

CALADENIA DILATATA (SPIDER ORCHID)

The large-flowered *Pterostylis baptistii* is one of the larger species, widespread from southern Queensland, New South Wales, and Victoria, where it grows in dense colonies in forests in damp conditions. Larger plants reach 24in (60cm) tall and are topped by a single large green-and-white flower.

Thelymitras are less easily cultivated and do not proliferate in the manner of greenhoods. However, some of the species are extremely decorative, none more so than the Queen of Sheba orchid, *Thelymitra variegata*, from Western Australia, where it grows among low shrubs and grass tussocks in sandy soils. Plants reach 16in (40cm) tall and bear a few irridescent flowers, in a mixture of red, yellow, and violet. Its leaf is slender and is unusual in being held in a spiral.

THELYMITRA VARIEGATA (SUN ORCHID)

Underground orchids

RHIZANTHELLA GARDNERI, a most extraordinary orchid from Western Australia, completes its life cycle underground. RHIZANTHELLA GARDNERI only reveals its daisy-like head above ground when it is time to pollinate, making it a very rare species that is seldom seen.

RHIZANTHELLA GARDNERI

HARDY ORCHIDS

THERE ARE A NUMBER OF ATTRACTIVE terrestrial orchids that will flower well in temperate climates in the open. They flower between spring and summer, set seed in late summer and fall, and die down in winter. Some like the lady's-slipper orchid, *Cypripedium*, are completely hardy. The position they prefer in the garden depends on their native habitat. Some species of *Dactylorhiza* do well in a woodland setting, while *Orchis* and *Ophrys* grow well in lawns, provided the grass is not cut early in the year.

DACTYLORHIZA PRAETEMISSA

OPHRYS LUTEA

European orchids

Some of the European orchids have proved easier to grow than had previously been thought possible. In particular, the marsh orchids of the genus *Dactylorhiza* are good garden plants that will form large clumps in suitable conditions. One of the best of these is *Dactylorhiza elata,* which produces 24in (60cm) tall stems topped by cylinders or pyramids of rich-purple flowers. It is native to southern France, Spain, and Northwest Africa, where it grows in wet meadows and marshes. *Dactylorhiza praetermissa* is another common marshland orchid from northwest Europe, distinguised by its unspotted leaves and bright-purple flowers.

The bee orchids of the genus *Ophrys* have intrigued generations of orchid lovers, but have proved tricky to grow. They are best grown in pots in a well-drained neutral or somewhat alkaline compost. The pretty yellow bee orchid, *O. lutea*, is a common Mediterranean species, the best forms of which come from Spain. It is usually a small plant, seldom more than 10in (25cm) tall, with a few beelike flowers at the top of the spike.

Species of *Orchis* are also difficult to grow in cultivation and are best tried in pots in an alpine glasshouse.

48

Pleione Alishan
This is a recently created hybrid,
one of whose parents is the
attractive P. FORMOSANA from
Taiwan (see page 50).

CYPRIPEDIUM CALCEOLUS

CYPRIPEDIUM FORMOSANUM

PLEIONE FORRESTII

Slipper orchids

The temperate slipper orchids belong to the genus *Cypripedium*, which comprises about 45 species distributed throughout northern temperate regions of the Old and New Worlds. In China, the center of diversity of the genus, they are found as far south as Yunnan, while in the New World *C. irapeanum* grows in Mexico and Guatemala.

The lady's-slipper orchid, *Cypripedium calceolus*, which is widespread in Europe, northern Asia and North America, has one or two yellow flowers with chocolate or rusty sepals and petals. The North American *C. reginae*, which grows in swampy conditions, is one of the best species in cultivation, forming large clumps in suitable conditions. Its stem can reach 24in (60cm) and carries an attractive white flower with a large pink lip.

One of the most unusual species in the genus is *C. formosanum* from Taiwan, where it grows in the mountain forests. It has fan-shaped leaves and a showy pink flower with a large inflated lip.

Windowsill orchids

The popularity of the small genus *Pleione*, comprising some 16 species from the Himalayas and China, has recently received a boost because of the introduction of the bright-yellow *P. forrestii* into cultivation and breeding programs. Most of the other species have purple, pink or white flowers, the best known being the pink-flowered *P. formosana* from Taiwan. *Pleione* Alishan is a recently created hybrid of *P. formosana* (see page 49). *Pleione forrestii* is a native of Yunnan Province of southwest China, where it grows in the mountains.

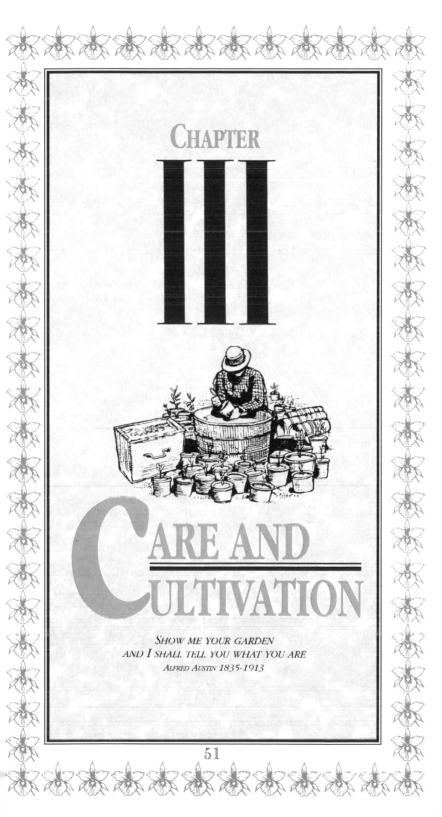

CHAPTER

III

CARE AND CULTIVATION

*SHOW ME YOUR GARDEN
AND I SHALL TELL YOU WHAT YOU ARE*
ALFRED AUSTIN 1835-1913

INTRODUCTION

ORCHIDS ARE DIFFERENT BUT NOT DIFFICULT. Most cultivated orchids are surprisingly capable of withstanding bad or indifferent growing conditions for prolonged periods. They need regular, but not constant, attention. Basically, you must ensure that orchids have adequate light, correct humidity levels, a well-drained open compost, and the correct watering regime (not excessive – orchids will tolerate occasional dryness far better than constant waterlogging). Orchids can be grown in every garden environment. From the open garden, through cold alpine-house conditions, to the steamy confines of the classical hothouse, there are orchids for each and every situation.

Orchids for the garden

Under this heading are included orchids that will survive winters in cool, temperate latitudes, where winter minimum temperatures of around 15°F (-10°C) may be expected. Most dependable garden orchids come from woodland conditions, and thrive in semi-shade, in well-drained moisture-retentive soils. Genera suitable for these conditions include *Cypripedium*, *Calanthe*, *Dactylorhiza* (also good in open situations), and *Epipactis*. *Bletilla* is one of the best orchids for a warm, open situation, thriving especially well at the foot of a wall.

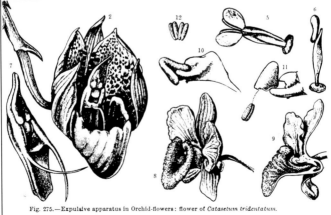

Fig. 275.—Expulsive apparatus in Orchid-flowers: flower of *Catasetum tridentatum*.

An illustration from THE NATURAL HISTORY OF PLANTS *1904, explaining the expulsive pollinating apparatus of orchid flowers.*

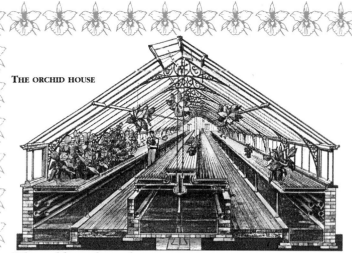

The cold or alpine house

This heading also includes cold-frame culture. Plants in these conditions are protected from the extremes of winter cold and, more importantly, from extremes of winter wet. All orchids suitable for the open garden thrive under these conditions, with the addition of winter-growing terrestrials from southern Europe, and some of the hardier Australian terrestrials in genera such as *Pterostylis*. The final major group for these conditions is the pleiones, many of which will survive temperatures of 20°F (-6°C) if dry.

The cool house

Cool-house conditions mimic those of the sub-tropics, or of high altitudes in the tropics proper. Winter-night minimum temperatures of 50°F (10°C), falling on the coldest nights to 45°F (6°C), are perfect for groups such as *Cymbidium* and the cooler-growing *Odontoglossum* species and hybrids. The former require lower relative humidity levels than the latter, and will also tolerate higher maximum temperatures. Odontoglossums should not be kept at temperatures in excess of 80°F (26°C) for long periods. Both groups do well in cool summer-night temperatures. Cool-growing slipper orchids, such as

Paphiopedilum insigne, also thrive here, as do many other genera – for example, *Dendrobium nobile* hybrids, disas, and numerous high-altitude *Coelogyne* species.

The intermediate house

Perhaps the widest range of tropical orchids can be accommodated in houses with night temperatures between 55 and 60°F (13-15°C). By varying the light regime, groups as diverse as the *Cattleya* alliance (which appreciate high light levels nearer the glass) and paphiopedilums (mainly forest-floor dwellers, luxuriating in shade) can be accommodated within the same house. Many genera, too numerous to mention, thrive in intermediate conditions.

The warm greenhouse

The warm house has conditions that come closest to the hothouse of yesteryear. Minimum night temperatures of 66-68°F (19-20°C) enable genera such as *Phalaenopsis* (the moth orchid) to thrive. Under these conditions vandaceous orchids, e.g. the imposing *Vanda*, and the smaller but colorful *Ascocenda*, will also do well. Imposing tropical terrestrials such as *Calanthe triplicata*, and the wonderful comet orchid, *Angraecum sesquipedale*, are also at home in the warm greenhouse.

Greenhouses

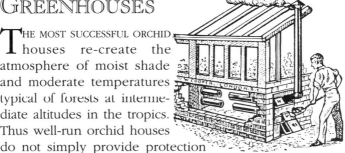

THE MOST SUCCESSFUL ORCHID houses re-create the atmosphere of moist shade and moderate temperatures typical of forests at intermediate altitudes in the tropics. Thus well-run orchid houses do not simply provide protection from cold winter temperatures, they also protect plants from other extremes, such as excessive heat, dry atmosphere, and excessive light. In the northern hemisphere, the best light conditions are obtained from greenhouses that are oriented east-west, with the long side facing south. Optimal growing conditions for most orchids require the correct balance between light, heat, and humidity, obtained by a judicious mixture of heating, shading, ventilation, and humidification.

Heating

The most commonly used heating systems for orchids use piped hot water or hot air, fueled by gas, solid fuel or electricity. Piped hot water is the best system, as the relatively large surface area of pipework around the orchid house ensures that heat is distributed very evenly. Hot-air heaters are cheaper and easier to install, but require fan assistance unless there is some form of ducting to take the heated air around the house. Electric fan heaters, which are extremely easy to install, are the most popular heat source for many growers. Whatever heat source you choose, fumes from the fuel must be vented externally, as they can rapidly build up to toxic levels.

Ventilation, shading, & air circulation

Ventilation and shading are closely linked in the effort to maintain equable growing conditions for orchids throughout the year, especially during hot weather. Orchids enjoy a buoyant atmosphere, and ventilation should be provided to relieve the stagnant conditions that prevail in many humid well-insulated greenhouses.

Orchids will grow well in most standard greenhouses or conservatories, although increasing the area of ventilation from the standard 15 percent of floor area to around 30 percent will allow for better ventilation without drafts.

Effective shading is crucial to maintain the balance between temperature and humidity required by most orchids. Shading helps to slow heat gain in orchid houses during sunny weather, reducing the need for ventilation, which assists in keeping a humid microclimate for the plants. Shading may be provided by proprietary shade paints, netting, laths or blinds. The most efficient systems are nets, laths or blinds, providing a 50 percent shade factor, fixed to the outside of the house with an insulating air gap, around 8-10in (20-25cm), between the shading and cladding. These systems can be adjusted or removed in dull weather, so that plants receive optimum light levels. However, healthy plants can be grown in houses where shading stays on all summer. Shade paints applied directly to the cladding are less efficient, but cheaper.

In areas that experience very high summer temperatures, effective cooling may be possible only with the assistance of wet pads and fans. These draw warm air in from outside through one end of the house and cool it by passing it across a wet pad, to replace hot air exhausted from the house at the opposite end.

Humidity

The term relative humidity (r.h.) refers to the amount of water the air may hold as vapor at any given temperature. As the air temperature increases so does its ability to absorb water, and without input from humidification the r.h. will fall. While the humidity requirement of orchids varies according to their original habitat, most fall between 50 and 80 percent r.h. The r.h. within an orchid house will vary between these limits over the course of a day, being at its lowest during the hottest period and at its highest overnight. Required humidity levels can be obtained by damping down floors and benches regularly, or by using automatic humidifiers.

Growing orchids indoors

MOST ORCHIDS CAN BE GROWN INDOORS. Enthusiasts may go to the trouble of creating special growing rooms, where, by using supplementary lighting and humidification, great success can be achieved. Smaller lighting rigs can be accommodated in a room, or a light (but not sunny) window. Terrariums with a completely enclosed growing environment can also be most attractive additions to indoor decor, and may be purchased from specialist manufacturers. Finally, and most simply, there are a number of orchids that grow perfectly well when treated as house plants.

For the ordinary grower who wishes to have orchids flowering in the house, there are two groups that can be guaranteed to succeed, given the sort of green thumb required by the average house plant. For year-round flowering the moth orchid, or *Phalaenopsis,* is the best candidate. This bears spikes of flowers in white, pink, and yellow, and may flower for many months from a single inflorescence. To grow moth orchids, you need a minimum night temperature of around 60°F (15°C), a light position near a window (but not direct sunlight), and an increase in relative humidity around the plants by growing them in pots standing on a tray of wet gravel. Small room humidifiers may also be used to moisten the atmosphere around the plants.

The other group of orchids that flower well indoors are the pleiones, or windowsill orchids. These small deciduous plants may be kept in a cool, dry place after their leaves fall in mid-autumn (anywhere frost-free will do), and brought into gentle heat (say a window in a room heated to no more than around 45°F (8-10°C) after the turn of the year. The flowers will emerge rapidly, and when they are beginning to open they can be placed in a warmer room, although they last better under cool conditions. As they start into growth, they may be moved into a frame or cool orchid house.

Composts & Containers

ORCHIDS GROW IN A GREAT VARIETY OF HABITATS, from terrestrial to epiphytic and from permanently moist to seasonally dry. A number of approaches may, therefore, be required to accommodate the demands of a mixed collection. However, most of the basic rules outlined here apply to the vast majority of orchids. The most important of these is the need for excellent drainage and aeration of their composts. Although orchids may occur naturally in very wet habitats, the niches they occupy (for example, perches on tree branches) ensure that water passes through their root systems rapidly, rather than stagnating around them for prolonged periods. Most orchids also undergo a regular wet/dry cycle, as water is lost very rapidly from their tree-branch habitats, and their open humus-rich soils then become well aerated. Working with this cycle forms the basis of successful traditional cultivation methods, particularly when plants are grown in containers.

Slabs or pots

Most cultivated orchids are either epiphytic species or have been bred from them, and will grow reasonably well when mounted on a piece of bark (known as a slab). But for most orchids, the best and most dependable results are undoubtedly obtained from growing in pots.

However, many growers prefer slabs for those orchids whose habit of growth makes them difficult to grow in pots (for example *Bulbophyllum* and *Aerangis*). Cork is the most commonly used bark, although other species, particularly hardwoods such as oak or apple, have been used with success. Plants should be mounted upon a thin layer of organic matter (fern fiber or moss) to provide a reservoir of moisture. A healthy and vigorous mounted plant, growing very much in the manner nature intended, gives a much better idea of how orchids live in the wild than do its potted counterparts.

Container types

Growing orchids in containers is the simplest method. There are various types, principally pots (clay or plastic) and baskets (wood or plastic). The type of container you choose will depend mainly on the habit of the plant, although personal preference also plays a part.

Composts

Orchids will thrive in a wide range of growing media, provided that growers understand the management of the plants in the compost provided. The underlying principles, as ever, are of great importance, and of these the most important is that orchid composts must be well structured – that is, they need to drain rapidly, allowing air to permeate the mix fairly quickly after watering. The range of materials in which orchids will thrive is remarkable, covering both the organic and inorganic. Orchids grow well in composts as diverse as volcanic scoria, pine and fir bark, fern fiber, sphagnum moss, moss peat, coconut husks, and even ultra-modern growing systems using rockwool (spun volcanic rock, not dissimilar to roof-insulation material).

It may sound contradictory, but while orchid composts should be well drained, they should also be moisture-retentive. The amount of water held by finer composts will be greater than that held by ones with a coarser particle size.

As orchid composts age, their organic constituents decay, slowly reducing the porosity of the mix. Many growers use inert fillers, such as perlite, perlag or charcoal, in an effort to retain the open nature of the mix. This lengthens the life of the compost, so that repotting owing to compost breakdown can be reduced. Peat-based mixes may last as little as six to nine months; small-grade bark mixes,

58

average size ¼in (6mm), will last a year to 18 months; and larger-grade barks can last for two years, or more in the case of the largest grade 1in (2.5cm) upwards.

The nutritional qualities of orchid mixes are not of such great importance as for other plants, as most of the feeding will be in a dilute form during the growing season. Most orchids grow in humus-rich acidic environments, and a compost pH of around 5.8-6.0 suits them well.

Standard compost mixes

The major consideration when choosing a compost mix is whether the orchid is epiphytic or terrestrial. The size of the plant and the fineness or otherwise of its root system are also of importance in deciding the grade of mix to use. While there is no definitive last word on orchid composts (and they change constantly as techniques evolve and new materials are introduced), mixes based upon bark, peat, and perlite are very popular and successful. A ratio of 3:3:2 of bark (pine, fir, or other conifer), peat (sphagnum-moss peat for preference), and perlite ('super-coarse' grade) is appropriate for a very wide range of tropical orchids, epiphytes and terrestrials alike.

The size and type of plant will dictate the particle size of the compost. Seedlings and very fine-rooted species (e.g. *Masdevallia*) grow well in composts with a particle size of about ¼in (6mm). Larger plants, such as mature cattleyas and other specimen plants, will grow better in mixes with a particle size of ¾in (19mm) and upwards.

In order to boost plants after repotting, add 2oz to 8 gallons (50gm to 36 liters) of fertilizer as a base dressing, with a ratio of 5:7.5:10 of the major nutrients N:P:K: (nitrogen:phosphorous:potash), and dolomite limestone (magnesium carbonate) at the same rate.

Potting orchids

ORCHIDS REQUIRE REPOTTING if the plant has outgrown its container or the compost has deteriorated. They are best repotted as they come into growth, typically in spring in temperate latitudes. The orchids themselves provide the most reliable guide. Those that grow along a rhizome (such as cymbidiums, cattleyas, paphiopedilums, and odontoglossums), should be repotted just as their new shoots emerge from the ends of last year's growths. Orchids without rhizomes (such as vandas and ascocendas) are ready for potting when there is renewed growth from their growing points, and new root tips.

How to pot

Remove plants very carefully from their old containers. Discard old compost, along with dead and diseased roots. The size of the new pot should reflect both the size of the plant above ground, and the amount of healthy roots present. Position the plant in the pot with enough room for the new growths to develop. Plants with growths all round should be placed centrally, while those that grow strongly in one direction (for example, many cattleyas) may be placed to one side of the pot with enough room in front of the leading bulb for next year's growth. Most rhizomatous orchids (cymbidiums, cattleyas, etc) should be planted with the rhizome around ¹/₂in (13mm) below the surface of the compost. Vandaceous orchids can be placed in their containers with the old bare stem at the base sunk into the compost. When the plant is in position, compost can be poured into the pot, leaving no gaps. The compost should then be lightly firmed. If the plant requires support, it should be staked.

Potting terrestrial orchids

The recommendations (above) relate to epiphytic orchids, in effect the vast majority of orchids grown. The underlying principles governing the cultivation of most terrestrials are similar to those for epiphytes. However, a quantity of the old compost is carried over into the new mix (around 25 percent), in order to ensure that the mycorrhizal fungus is present.

The standard terrestrial orchid mix is as follows: 1 part clay loam (steam sterilized): 1 part sharp gritty sand: 1 part organic matter (comprising equal parts of screened oak/beech leafmold and fine-grade bark). To this mix add organic fertilizer, (dried blood and bone meal in equal parts) using 1 dessertspoonful per 2 gallons (10ml per 9 liters) of compost.

Terrestrial orchids should be repotted as they come into growth. Winter-dormant species should be repotted in early spring. Tubers and rhizomes of terrestrial species should be set around 1-1¹/₂in (2.5-4cm) below the surface of the compost.

FERTILIZERS & FEEDING

ORCHIDS ARE ADAPTED TO NUTRIENT-POOR HABITATS, and thus require less feeding than most other plants. The golden rule when feeding orchids is to use "little and often"; and the most effective formulations are liquid feeds, used at low concentrations. Specially formulated orchid feeds are also available, but in their absence ordinary liquid fertilizers may be used at around half the lowest recommended strength.

When to feed

Frequency of feeding depends upon the season of the plant's phase of growth. During winter, feeding may be reduced to almost nothing during the shortest days, with one feed at every three waterings before and after this period. During the growing season, when the plants are making new growth strongly, feed may be given at alternate waterings.

Watering

Most orchids come from areas where the water is acidic, and both acid-neutral water from a faucet and rainwater are quite safe to use for irrigation. Hard water may lead to problems with orchids, although the very acid bark- and peat-based composts used by orchid growers can alleviate hard water conditions. Never use domestic water softeners. Water can be safely softened by using a de-ionizer, or by adding phosphoric acid to stored water in a butt, to get the pH down to between 6 and 6.5.

Frequency of watering

Experience alone will teach you how frequently to water orchids, but the theory is very simple. The most important rule is to ensure that orchids have a definite wet/dry cycle. Orchids growing on slabs, in open baskets or in slatted pots require more regular watering than those in solid containers. Watering frequency should be reduced considerably during the winter. The plants themselves provide the best guide to their requirements. However, orchids cannot be relied upon to wilt when dry. The best way to check whether a plant needs watering is to lift the pot; if the compost is dry, it will be distinctly light or top-heavy. If that is the case, then the plant should be watered thoroughly, then left to become fairly dry again. If in doubt, do not water until the next day. This method works well for epiphytes, and thus for the great majority of orchids in cultivation. Terrestrials in loam-based composts require a more even moisture regime during their growth phase, and should not be allowed to dry out as much as epiphytes.

Pests & Diseases

ORCHIDS CAN SUFFER from much the same pests and diseases that afflict other plants, and the methods of controlling them are much the same. Very few conditions will cause the rapid demise of a healthy plant, and prompt action when signs or symptoms are spotted will often save the day. Bad cultivation techniques can lead to disease problems, especially fungi and rot associated with poor compost and waterlogged conditions. So it pays to check that plants are in good condition at the roots before considering other causes of decline or ill-health.

Pests

There are two major groups: those that damage plants by biting, and those that cause damage by sucking. Among the former are slugs and snails, thrips, weevils, and cockroaches; and among the latter, aphids, mealy bugs, scale insects, and mites. You can control these pests using the usual remedies sold by garden centers. Chemicals such as the pyrethroids, derris, malathion, metaldehyde, diazinon, and dicofol are all safe to use on orchids. New formulations should be tested on a limited number of plants before using them on an entire collection.

Diseases

Fungal and bacterial diseases occur most often when growing conditions are not quite right, especially in still, dank conditions. Control is to some degree by cultural means, by drying off the plants, improving airflow around them, and cutting out all affected tissues. The latter method is not always possible with fungi, which might attack many parts of the plant at once. The presence of bacteria is easy to detect, owing to the soft rots they cause and their rather offensive odor. Fungi can also cause rots, often characterized by a purple stain around the infected area. There are also numerous leafspot fungi – not usually fatal, but often unsightly.

In addition to good culture, diseases can be controlled by using Physan (for bacteria and fungi, especially rots). Leafspot fungi can be controlled by preventative sprays. Substances such as benomyl, zineb, and ferbam are safe to use on orchids.

The worst orchid diseases are caused by viruses. Infection can lead to deformation, with black and brown streaking of foliage and flowers, plus the general deterioration of the plant, leading sometimes to its death. There are no controls for viruses, and you should discard any plants that appear to be infected. Viruses are spread principally by growers using the same tools to cut into the living tissues of a number of orchids. Cleaning blades between cuts by inserting them in a propane-torch flame will assist in controling virus spread.

PROPAGATION

GROWING ORCHIDS FROM SEED is normally a technical operation, not usually undertaken by amateurs. Most orchids are propagated either by division (for the rhizomatous types) or by cuttings (for the vandaceous types). Division of orchids is broadly similar to that of other herbaceous plants. For best results, divide plants when they start to come into growth, usually as they are being repotted. Make sure that all divisions have a growing point and that they are not too small. Typically, a growing point and two previous years' growths behind it will constitute a viable division.

Cuttings of vandaceous orchids should consist of a piece of stem with active roots, and three or more pairs of leaves below the growing point. Vandaceous-orchid cuttings may be as much as 12in (30cm) or more long, whereas with the smaller species they are scarcely 1in (2.5cm) in length.

Buying seedlings is a relatively cheap way to build a collection. Very young seedlings should be grown together in 3-4in (8-10cm) half-pots, planted about ½in (13mm) apart. Provide close, humid conditions initially; then as they become established, replant them in individual pots.

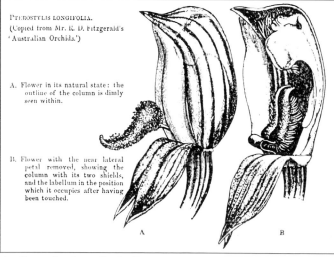

PTEROSTYLIS LONGIFOLIA.
(Copied from Mr. R. D. Fitzgerald's 'Australian Orchids.')

A. Flower in its natural state: the outline of the column is dimly seen within.

B. Flower with the near lateral petal removed, showing the column with its two shields, and the labellum in the position which it occupies after having been touched.

A   B

An illustration from Charles Darwin's **FERTILISATION OF ORCHIDS 1904**.

REFERENCES

There are many manuals for orchid growers,
many of which are quite excellent.
The author's select list below covers most of the information
that the beginner and the more advanced grower
could wish to know.

Home Orchid Growing, Rebecca Northen.
Very much the Bible for serious growers – recently revised.
Published by Van Nostrand Rheinhold (USA) 1991
Manual of Cultivated Orchid Species, Bechtel, Cribb and Launert.
The best identification guide to orchid species,
including much background information on the plants illustrated,
(now in its third edition).
Published by the Blandford Press (UK) 1992
Hardy Orchids, Phillip Cribb & Christopher Bailes.
The only guide to orchids for the garden and frost-free greenhouse.
Published by Christopher Helm (UK) 1989
Orchids and how to grow them, Christopher Bailes.
An inexpensive introductory guide to all aspects of orchid growing.
Published by The Eric Young Orchid Foundation 1987

ACKNOWLEDGMENTS

The producers gratefully acknowledge the following individuals,
organizations, and sources that have assisted in the
creation of this book.

FOR THE CREATION OF ORIGINAL ILLUSTRATIONS:
JULIA COBBOLD
FOR THE COLORING & ENHANCEMENT OF ARCHIVE ILLUSTRATIONS:
Robin Harris & David Day
FOR THE SUPPLY OF PHOTOGRAPHS :
Dr. Phillip Cribb, The Orchid Herbarium,
The Royal Botanic Gardens, Kew, Richmond, Surrey, TW9 3AE, UK.
FOR PICTORIAL REFERENCES AND VISUAL MATERIAL:
The Natural History of Plants, Kerner & Oliver,
The Gresham Publishing Co. 1904
The Gardener's Assistant, William Watson
The Gresham Publishing Co. 1908
Fertilisation of Orchids, Charles Darwin,
John Murray 1904
The Dover Pictorial Archive series
Botanical Prints, Norman & Eve Robinson
Studio Editions 1990
The Gardeners' and Poultry Keepers' Guide & Catalogue,
William Cooper 1900